Appraising job Performance

How to improve job satisfaction
and organisational success

Patrick Forsyth

howto books

Practical books that inspire

Organising a Conference
How to plan and run a successful event

Successful Negotiating
Getting what you want in the best possible way

Make Meetings Work
How to prepare and run a meeting
to get the results you want

Train Your Team Yourself
How to deliver effective in-house training

Writing a Report
How to prepare, write and present powerful reports

howtobooks

Please send for a free copy of the latest catalogue:

HowTo Books
3 Newtec Place, Magdalen Road,
Oxford OX4 1RE, United Kingdom
info@howtobooks.co.uk
www.howtobooks.co.uk

Appraising Job Performance

Published by How To Books Ltd,
3 Newtec Place, Magdalen Road,
Oxford OX4 1RE. United Kingdom.
Tel: (01865) 793806. Fax: (01865) 248780.
info@howtobooks.co.uk
www.howtobooks.co.uk

British Library Cataloguing in Publication Data.
A catalogue record for this book is available from
the British Library.

Cover design by Baseline Arts Ltd, Oxford
Produced for How To Books by Deer Park Productions
Typeset by PDQ Typesetting, Newcastle-under-Lyme, Staffs.
Printed and bound by Bell & Bain Ltd, Glasgow

NOTE: The material contained in this book is set out in good faith for
general guidance and no liability can be accepted for loss or expense
incurred as a result of relying in particular circumstances on statements
made in the book. Laws and regulations are complex and liable to change,
and readers should check the current position with the relevant authorities
before making personal arrangements.

Contents

Preface

'It's what you learn after you know it all that counts.'

John Wooden

Managers want to get the best performance from their staff; and there are many aspects of management that are designed to help achieve just that – motivation, development, consultation and more. If ongoing efforts are being made to ensure good performance, then it is sensible to have regular checks to see how things are going. This is important to managers; and also to staff, who normally like to know how their performance is rated.

Hence the appraisal. Sometimes given grander-sounding names – job performance appraisal or evaluation – this is essentially a meeting, often an annual meeting, to check how things are going and to link to the future. In many organisations the process involved has a certain amount of formality attached to it, and is bound up with other factors such as salary review.

Sounds fine. And yet it is an area that is too often less than successful. Managers often dread conducting such meetings, finding the process a chore or difficult or awkward to do. Members of staff often come out of appraisal meetings feeling they were not useful or constructive or, worse, that they were unfair or unreasonable.

Yet appraisals represent a significant *opportunity* for managers and staff alike. They should be useful, and they are a specific opportunity to enhance motivation and make good performance in the following period more certain. So they need to be made effective. This book is aimed at everyone who must conduct performance appraisals of their staff. It sets out the essentials – the key approaches and techniques that really matter – and is designed to help you make such meetings easier to conduct, more likely to be appreciated by your people and, above all, more likely to maximise their future performance.

Patrick Forsyth

Touchstone Training & Consultancy
28 Saltcote Maltings
Maldon
Essex CM9 4QP
United Kingdom

1 · Reasons To Appraise

The rationale – why appraisal is necessary to both managers and their staff

In this Chapter:

1 MANAGEMENT
RESPONSIBILITIES

---

2 BENEFITS FOR MANAGERS

---

3 FOCUSING ON STAFF

---

4 FUTURE CHALLENGES

---

1 · MANAGEMENT RESPONSIBILITIES

Managers are charged with obtaining results. Often these link directly or indirectly to the finances of the organisation for which they work, but they may involve numbers of different things: productivity, efficiency, and so on and may also be measured in a variety of ways.

Management, to define it simply, is about getting results through other people (and therefore not *for* them). It follows that whatever personal – executive – responsibilities a manager may have, their prime responsibility is for managing their team. It is upon their team's performance that they stand or fall.

People management involves a number of things and is essentially defined as consisting of six overriding tasks: recruitment and selection, planning and organisation of people and activities, motivation and development of the team and control of activities. Within this broad picture, of course, there are a variety of individual tasks that have to be undertaken either occasionally or regularly; and one such is appraisal. It is an integral part of the process of team maintenance and is specifically the personal responsibility of every line manager.

It is also a significant way of helping to ensure appropriate performance and of positively influencing people's motivation.

Defining terms

Between recruitment and the termination of employment there should come regular appraisals. These are usually annual, sometimes a little more frequent. They will be formal or informal; and the first may link to formal organisation-wide systems. All are a form of communication. All are an opportunity. This is so despite the fact that not everyone's experience of them is good, nor is conducting them something that every manager looks forward to doing. Indeed without the right approach they can be dissatisfying for all concerned. At worst they are seen as a time-consuming irrelevance that promises much and delivers nothing.

Let us define matters a little before going further. At its simplest appraisal means a manager answering the question 'How am I doing?' on behalf of a member of their staff. It presumes that there are guidelines as to what should be occurring and runs a rule over what is being done and how it is being done in order to improve performance in the future. It is a force for good in two ways, first by identifying and correcting gaps in peoples' skills and competencies, and secondly by helping them keep pace in a fast changing work and organisational environment. The proportion of the total task that seems to relate to the latter grows all the time.

It is a process that, in most organisations, has a formality to it, and we will touch on the systems that create this in due course. At its heart, though, it is a matter of individual communication between a manager and their staff, it is inextricably linked to the working relationship that exists between them, and it must be considered a prime responsibility of every manager. There may be many things that you can delegate, but appraisal of those reporting directly to you is not likely to be one of them. No matter; as was said in the Preface, appraisal is an opportunity. It is not something to be avoided, but something from which to obtain as many benefits as possible, not least because there are many different such benefits to be had.

2 · BENEFITS FOR MANAGERS

Why appraise?

There are many good reasons for reviewing performance. Most are very directly related to a person's work with and for their manager, but one is rather different so we will start with that.

For many managers the reason for holding appraisals is that it is a mandatory, and organisation-wide, process. Some of the reasons for this do not reflect a truly constructive view of appraisal.

One such purpose is to comply with employment legislation. Certainly this is so in the United Kingdom, and in other countries also (though legislation of course varies country by country). This is a powerful and sensible reason. Essentially what needs to be borne in mind here is that it is difficult to fire people for failing to perform adequately if they have not had any appraisal. If they take action and say dismissal is unfair they are likely to win;

how can performance be said to be inadequate if no one has ever told them things were not going well?

If an individual's performance really is inadequate and radical action is necessary, then remember that a series of formal warnings are necessary.

Worse is a situation of no job description and no appraisal – then they will say that they had no guidance regarding what they should do and no feedback on how they were doing it either. Anyone wanting to avoid wasting time and money should avoid industrial tribunals like the plague; hence appraisal systems exist in most organisation. If this sounds pretty cynical, perhaps it is – it is no reflection on the need for positive employment legislation, but certainly it is a lost opportunity to see appraisals being conducted only for negative reasons.

3 · **FOCUSING ON STAFF**

Good reasons

There are, of course, many positive reasons for appraisal. These include:

- reviewing an individual's past performance

- planning their future work and role

- setting specific individual goals for the future

- agreeing and creating individual ownership of such goals

- identifying development needs and setting up development activities

- on-the-spot coaching

- obtaining feedback

- reinforcing or extending the reporting relationship

- acting as a catalyst to delegation

- focusing on longer-term career progression

- acting to underpin or increase motivation.

It is a useful exercise to compile a list of factors that are specific to your own situation so that you can make sure that everything about the process relates to them.

Overall, the intention underlying all these kinds of thought is to ensure and improve future performance. Perhaps managers and staff each take a slightly different view of the benefits. Managers will perhaps see it primarily in terms of immediate performance improvement, while staff may most like to see it helping with development and assisting their prospects for increasing their responsibility or, ultimately, of promotion.

The good appraisal takes the view that even the best performance can be improved, and seeks to increase the likelihood of future work going to plan and future results being achieved as planned.

> *One can perhaps seek even more than this, as Scott Volkers said: The greatest pleasure in life is achieving things that people say can't be done.*

The link with remuneration

In the eyes of many people, and indeed in the way that many systems operate, there is an inextricable link between appraisal and salary review. In fact, most experts agree that a degree of distance is desirable. The objectives of appraisal are listed above. Of course the output of such discussions is useful in making assessments and decisions about salary (indeed about all aspects of the reward package). But the nature of the meeting can be compromised, and other discussions skimped, if the meeting is seen as a formality with the announcement at the end – so, we will be putting your salary up 6% – as being the only interesting part.

It is better, therefore, to separate the two things. An appraisal is just that, and salary discussions and announcements should be separate; though perhaps they are scheduled at a similar time of year. The detailed results of appraisal can easily suffer without this. The separation of appraisal and salary review is a principle that is worth establishing (or sticking with if this is already the way you operate). If currently the two things are handled together, then making a change may be seen as a retrograde step by staff who look forward to the remuneration discussion within the appraisal interview. A change, however desirable, needs some explaining and it certainly means making sure that the new, separate, appraisal is wholly constructive and useful in its own right. Once established, this separation prevents confusion, and maximises the effectiveness of both processes.

A range of people

Whom do you appraise? Normally it is the people who have a line-reporting relationship with you. Some may have worked with you for a while, in which case their appraisal should become an almost routine part of their overall activity. Some, everyone at some stage, may be new – newly recruited or moved in some way so that they now report to you. And some may, depending on your position, be senior, experienced, expert (and prima donna!). Everyone needs appraising and everyone can benefit from it, at least when it is done well. You do need to think, however, of the precise status of individuals and of the different approaches that may be necessary because of this.

4 · FUTURE CHALLENGES

One last point as this first chapter closes. Nothing can change the past, and appraisal is certainly not an exception. The prime idea is to look to the future and many of the details that follow here link to this principle. Of course things may have happened in the past which we want to prevent happening again, and there may be things that demand censure. The opportunity, however, is primarily one of influencing the future. Appraisal is a process of analysing past events and using the experience to help influence the achievement of future results.

IN SUMMARY

The key things to have in mind at this stage are that appraisal:

- Is necessary to organisational and personal success.

- Must be conducted in such a way as to make it valuable to staff and managers alike.

- Can make a real difference to results.

In a word it is an *opportunity*; and one that, as has been said, is significant.

2 · Preparation for Appraisal

Preparing carefully provides a sound foundation for a successful outcome.

In this Chapter:

1 UNDERSTANDING THE PROCESS
2 ENSURING READINESS IN OTHERS
3 PREPARING YOUR OWN ROLE
4 LINKING BACK

Ensuring that the opportunity of appraisal is forthcoming is not simply a question of conducting a good meeting. The success of any appraisal has its roots in the thinking and action that precedes it.

Thus, like so much else in management, the key to effective appraisals is preparation. This should not just be in the sense of preparation just ahead of the meeting, and it applies to both the appraiser and the appraisee. Consider the staff member first.

Skimping preparation almost always makes anything less effective. As Beverly Sills said: There are no shortcuts to any place worth going.

1 · UNDERSTANDING THE PROCESS

The first task is to ensure a basic understanding of the appraisal process and why it is necessary; without this it is difficult, if not impossible, for staff to prepare. So, the management communication job here is to create a constructive attitude amongst staff towards the whole process. Such communications can start as soon as people join an organisation and must be in evidence when appraisals are due. Appraisal should be a topic of every induction, indeed the way in which this is done can be planned and made a regular part of the process for every new member of staff. Beyond that, the specific tasks include:

- Explaining the rationale for appraisal

- Setting out the specific objectives of the process

- Making clear the measurement aspects

- Explaining the procedures and documentation

- Briefing as to what action is required of the appraisee

- Spelling out the advantages to both the organisation and the individual.

Only if both parties are clear regarding such a list are appraisals likely to be really useful. Once there is clarity in this respect, then the appraisal process can proceed. A systematic approach, and attention to detail, by the manager in both preparing and conducting appraisal meetings is still essential if the process is to be constructive.

A useful adjunct to explaining the process is a completed – sample – appraisal form; such can act as an example and do more than volumes of more general explanation.

At this point you can move onto the task of making the appraisal interview go well, still focusing on the preparation necessary for those to be appraised.

2 · ENSURING READINESS IN OTHERS

Every individual whose appraisal you will conduct should be encouraged to prepare. This will make the meeting more useful for you both, not least that the meeting itself will be easier to conduct.

The first step is to ensure that you communicate clearly and thoroughly the purpose and form of the scheduled appraisal. People should understand the need for it, appreciate its importance, and be aware of the specific objectives it addresses and how both parties can get the best from it. It is essential that people understand and are familiar with the system of appraisal and have copies of any documentation that must be used.

Beyond that, it is a good idea to suggest that people prepare throughout the year. This may entail action as simple as keeping an appraisal 'collection' file. In this people should note matters that can usefully be raised at appraisal and link these notes to the filing of copies of any documents that will assist the process. Without this action memory can be stretched to call to mind all the things that have occurred throughout a year and those that lend themselves to discussion at an appraisal. It can avoid opportunities for constructive discussion and review being missed. Such action needs little time on the way through the year, but it can end saving a significant amount of time when the actual process of appraisal begins.

You may want to set this up formally to be sure that it actually happens. You may also suggest that close to appraisal time people send you a preliminary note suggesting ideas for the agenda, and details that might usefully be touched on in the meeting.

Make sure also that there is adequate feedback about suggestions. You might get a request at any time of year about a subsequent appraisal meeting. Always reply promptly in whatever way is appropriate so that no loose ends are left exposed. This may simply involve an exchange of memos, or e-mails, or a meeting or discussion of some sort. It is important that, come the meeting, nothing can be raised and quoted as an earlier omission, or as having been ignored, making what is then done at the meeting incomplete or unfair.

A confident, well-prepared appraisee will be more likely to adopt a constructive attitude to the proceedings and this benefits the whole process.

Now, what about you?

3 · **PREPARING YOUR OWN ROLE**

As appraiser, you should likewise keep a file for each person who reports to you, and you should also plan in some detail the kind of meeting you intend to run. More of this in a moment.

As has been said any manager almost certainly needs a way of collecting information, and thoughts, about each member of their team throughout the year. Appraisal is the end point of a process that should span the year. Realistically it is difficult for most people to recall every detail of an individual's working year and the events – positive and negative – that comprised it (more so for several members of staff). Furthermore, being seen to be conducting an interview on the basis of incomplete information will cast the whole process in the wrong light, and at worst its credibility will be lost. So, you must:

■ Spend sufficient time with people throughout the year

■ Keep clear records

■ Brief people on their role and what to expect

■ Assimilate (and explain) the documentation and systems of
  appraisal

■ Prepare for each individual appraisal you will conduct.

*The importance of spending time with people
cannot be overestimated. Appraising staff with
whom you have had little contact during the year is
always going to be difficult.*

Clearly your role here overlaps with what has been said about
prompting members of staff to prepare. What some of the
time spent with people should consist of is touched on later
in this chapter. First we review the immediate preparation
task. Background information needs looking into. It may be
that this includes checking an appraisee's job description
(which may need amendment after the appraisal); looking

up specific objectives set for the past period; considering changes that have occurred or are planned for the job, its responsibilities or circumstances, that need to be taken into account. And, of course, linking back to any previous appraisal meeting held, and any relevant company or personal records.

Thereafter a systematic approach to getting ready for a meeting will assist the process. You may well need to think about what suits you best, and about what the system you use requires to be done (and to compromise between the two), but the following is intended to act as a guide to what might work best.

The system should not act like a straightjacket and prevent flexibility, it is more like a route map which can act to guide the way whatever the circumstances.

Before the appraisal interview

Steps that can help ensure a good meeting, and which need taking ahead of it, might include the following.

- **Prepare a written notification:** an explanatory note at this stage is the last chance to make sure people approach their appraisal in the right way. This means that as well as confirming a mutually convenient time and date, certain background information needs to be included as well (and perhaps copies of any documents or forms to be used or referred to during the meeting). This is also the time to issue an agenda, either complete or as a guide which may request feedback and suggestions.

- **Study the individual's file:** indeed go further if necessary, making sure that all information you need about what was supposed to be happening and what has happened is to hand. Make notes of points arising that need discussion and ensure that you can find your way around the file and documentation easily as the meeting progresses.

■ **Check performance factors:** for example, by referring to standards agreed and also to any aspects that are no longer relevant, or in need of amendment or addition.

■ **Draft a provisional assessment:** perhaps a page that will act as a starting point. Do not prejudge the discussion or make decisions which logically can only follow discussion. These notes may certainly influence the meeting agenda, and may also help you adapt a formal appraisal system to what best suits an individual.

■ **Critique your initial thoughts:** it is useful to ask yourself a firm 'Why?' question about anything said at this stage. If there is no clear answer that comes to mind, then more research may be necessary or otherwise the fact may influence the line the appraisal meeting needs to take. For example, if your initial judgement is that someone's time management is poor, asking 'Why do I feel that?' will lead logically to your seeking some tangible examples (and some indisputable facts) to demonstrate your case and make the point that action is needed in this area.

■ **Consider specific areas of the appraisal:** for instance consider development. It may be clear at this stage that some training is necessary after the appraisal meeting. Again without prejudging the issues, it may be useful to check out what might suit so that this can be incorporated into the discussion.

■ **Think ahead:** remember that the most important part of the discussion will be about the next period. It may be useful to plan particular projects and tasks for the future; especially perhaps those that foster development as well as simply reflect operational considerations. Thinking of relevant things as the discussion progresses may be difficult and what is raised needs to be, and must also be seen to be, well selected.

■ **Consult with others:** where this is necessary to a complete picture, it may be useful to consult with others about the person to be appraised; others who work with or who cross paths with them, from specialists like the Training Manager, to people in other sections or functions.

■ **Check the rationale of your intentions:** in other words, make sure that you are able to answer the appraisee's question 'Why?' about anything that you plan to raise and discuss.

Careful work and thought at this stage is invaluable. Appraisal is not the sort of activity in which you want to find yourself saying 'if only I had . . .' and having to continue in a way you know could have been better.

> *It may be useful to produce a personal checklist of all the things that must be done ahead of appraisals; keep it in your 'appraisal file' and use it ahead of the appraisal cycle.*

4 · LINKING BACK

Finally, let us return to the thought that immediate preparation is not something to be viewed in isolation, it should reflect ongoing contact from throughout the year. This should occur in two ways.

Routine day-to-day management contact: in other words, operational activity gives rise to contacts which then link to appraisal. For example, you might have a progress meeting to discuss matters linked to a specific project, and then find that matters arise with longer term implications for the general performance of an individual. Sometimes this might be minor. No discussion is necessary, but the event needs lodging away as part of the picture you have of those you appraise; maybe sometimes this warrants a written note in the file. Alternatively sometimes there can usefully be a formal digression. You label it as linked to appraisal, you discuss whatever it is and note it warrants further discussion in other informal sessions or in the next formal appraisal meeting.

Planned follow-up sessions: meetings that flow directly from the last formal appraisal. Take an example. If someone's development in presentational skills is addressed at appraisal time, part of the answer may be formal – sending them on a course perhaps. But part may be addressed by mentoring. Each time they have to make a presentation, you schedule a little time to assist with or monitor their preparation and performance and these sessions, in turn, link to the next formal appraisal session. Such action need not be approached piecemeal; it can be planned ahead. You flag and agree the need, you identify future activity that links to presentations and you schedule a series of actions across a period that will assist in improving the situation. The power of this link between appraisal and ongoing informal, and perhaps very simple, low-cost, and non time-consuming action should never be underestimated. It is precisely this sort of working together between management and staff that can make the relationship productive and help to ensure results are achieved.

In all such cases, there is continuity involved, as specific preparations that lock in ahead of the next formal appraisal time.

IN SUMMARY

The key thing about preparation is simply to resolve to do it. Approached systematically it need not be time consuming, indeed it may well save future time on other aspects of the process. Particularly:

■ Recognise that preparation involves both parties in the appraisal situation.

■ Ensure that you instigate a process of preparation that spans the year, as well as getting yourself organised just before the meeting.

■ Ensure you undertake any necessary research and checking that will put you in a position to do the best job.

On the day a well-prepared appraiser will always be able to make those they appraise feel that justice is being done to the process, and that it is important and worthwhile.

3 · Setting Up the Interview

Creating the circumstances for an acceptable, and thus successful, appraisal meeting.

In this Chapter:

1 MAXIMISING THE OPPORTUNITY

2 MAKING IT CONSTRUCTIVE

Appraisals should be viewed positively; even so they are likely to prompt at least some feelings of apprehension amongst those about to be appraised (and perhaps amongst appraisers also!). In the interests of both efficiency and courtesy you should set the meeting up in such a way as to do it justice. Some of the first points here may seem obvious but all are important – and, in a busy world, such matters can easily be handled in a way that is less than ideal.

So, you can usefully bear in mind the following.

1 · MAXIMISING THE OPPORTUNITY

Time and duration

Allow enough time: both to do the job and to give the right impression about the occasion. Few appraisals will be accomplished properly in less than an hour, some may last two or three hours (or more) and still be time usefully spent. Skimping the time is a false economy. People will resent it if they do not 'get their say' and will also feel that more time would have resolved negative issues about which they may have been left feeling bad.

Do not let the fact that you may have a number of people whose appraisals you must conduct, which all together will take up some time, allow you to short change any individual.

Pick an appropriate moment: it should suit both parties and fit in with other activities, allowing sufficient time beforehand for preparation, and not clashing with other activities that would make concentration difficult. The precise time set is important too. A time that necessitates an early start, runs over lunch or on into the evening may be unsuitable, though this will depend on the people, the culture and how jobs normally work.

Schedule the time and place well ahead: give people plenty of notice and make sure that you, and the designated place (if, say, you have to book a meeting room) remain free.

Organise the right environment

Create a suitable environment: appraisals should be held somewhere comfortable, perhaps less formally than across a desk, yet with all the facilities required, for example:

- comfortable chairs (easy, perhaps, rather than upright)

- perhaps with table or desk space to lay out papers and/or cups and saucers

- no distracting noise

- clear confidentiality (i.e. no one can overhear)

- any refreshments arranged, and announced, in advance

- good light

- a manageable number of people present (if other senior people are present – other than the line manager – their role should be explained and the layout should reflect it – for example, an observer can sit a little way back)

■ a clear, and announced, level of formality (e.g. can you take your jacket off?)

■ necessary equipment to hand or arrangements made for things like photocopying (or maybe you need a flipchart or similar).

Allow no disturbances: nothing will more quickly give people the impression that you do not rate the event highly than allowing constant, or even occasional, pauses while you, say, take telephone calls.

Always switch off those modern annoyances – any mobile phone or paging devices.

Leave clear instructions with secretaries, switch-boards or voice-mail systems – and stick to them. Short of a major crisis, what is more important than the opportunity to maximise the future performance of your people?

Plan to put the individual at their ease: recognise

that, even with good communication beforehand, appraisals may be viewed as somewhat traumatic occasions. Everything that can be done to counter this (which includes some of the above) is useful and should be pre-arranged.

Make a distinction between staff having their first appraisal and subsequent ones: familiarity, and good experience of appraisals, will make the process seem less daunting; indeed people should look forward to them. Those approaching the matter for the first time deserve, and may need, more time.

All these kinds of consideration allow the focus to be on the right things.

Documentation

There is a variety of documentation associated with appraisals, and some very simple, but important, rules apply here.

Read everything necessary in advance: you need to have, and to demonstrate, a familiarity with things, whether this is the system or the detail of some particular event to be discussed. You may want to emphasise the importance of doing likewise to appraisees, and perhaps even to check that it has been done. Having a segment of the appraisal meeting disrupted because some document has not been read – where perhaps a pause becomes necessary – plays havoc with the timing of the meeting. It is possible also that some appraisees may claim not to have read something in order to avoid a discussion about it; another reason to be sure ahead of the meeting that this has been done.

This is sufficiently important to warrant a formal system. You do not want to be constantly checking up on staff, but here the importance justifies both parties recognising the need to make sure it happens.

Copy papers in advance: if there are things both parties need these should be copied and, as has already been said, distributed in advance. Decide how you will complete documentation: for example, if an appraisal form needs completion will this be done during the meeting, be formulated in draft during the meeting to tidy up later or will notes be made for subsequent transcription onto a form?

Always have a clear agenda: both as a courtesy and a convenience this is essential; and it needs providing in advance.

Support material

You should think through the details of anything else you may need to have to hand during the meeting. Such may include straightforward things like your diary (you may want to schedule follow-up sessions), and you may want to prompt the appraisee to bring such things to the meeting also. You may want to include visual aids; even something as simple as a carefully prepared graph may demonstrate a point and focus discussion in the right way, when a long list of figures might cause delay and argument by being less clear.

Incidentally, look at your own circumstances in this respect. It

may be less than credible to be hectoring someone for being dis-
organised if they can hardly see you over the clutter and chaos on
your desk!

2 · MAKING IT CONSTRUCTIVE

Other people

Often appraisal means simply a session between a manager
and an immediate subordinate. Sometimes there is a third
party present, maybe the next up the management chain or
a specialist such as someone from a Personnel or Human
Resources department (and occasionally both, though mob-
handed appraisal is not usually recommended and can dilute
effectiveness).

If the decision is up to you, then the first job is to think about
who exactly should be present (and also who should not be
there). If the system of appraisal dictates those to be
involved then you move straight on to the second job: briefing them and agreeing roles.

■ Make sure they have, and have read, in advance all necessary papers.

■ Meet with them ahead of the meeting itself and agree who will do what and who will be in the chair (remember only one person can do that); do not try to do this by telephone, for example, if a meeting is really necessary to do it justice.

■ The direct responsibility for the appraisal of your people must be with you as line manager, so ideally the final decision about all such arrangements should be with you too; if necessary you must fight your corner to achieve what you regard as the best set-up.

It is so important to get things set up to create the best possible meeting that, if there are difficulties here, it may be worth postponing an appraisal until you are content that it is really set up well.

Clearly all these kinds of matters should be finalised a little in advance and some decisions made may form part of the information that you will need to pass on to the appraisee. Be careful to inform them not just about what is happening but why. The key thing from the appraisee's point of view is how it will affect them. You should be able to offer clear explanations, indeed if you cannot it may be a sign that a decision or arrangement needs a re-think.

On the day, any team of people must operate seamlessly. There is no room for hesitation which betrays a lack of preparation – 'I think that's all I had to say about that, the next question was John's, I think.' Not getting this aspect right risks diluting the effectiveness of the event, or at the least the appraisee's perception of it.

The proceedings during the meeting also need care. Clearly this is an area of a considerable range of detail. Appraisals will vary with the circumstances, not least the role and function of the individual being appraised. The next chapter takes us into the meeting itself.

IN SUMMARY

The preliminaries of the set-up of an appraisal involve four overall factors:

■ Timing

■ Environment

■ Documentation (and thus system)

■ People

The success of the actual appraisal meeting stems in part from this stage, it creates a solid foundation that can help make the event successful.

4 · Conducting the Interview

Conducting a meeting that directs both parties to play an appropriate part in the meeting.

In this Chapter:

1 CREATING STRUCTURE FOR THE MEETING

2 ENCOURAGING DISCUSSION

3 USING THE SYSTEM

4 AGREEING ACTION

1 · CREATING STRUCTURE FOR THE MEETING

The core of the appraisal process is, of course, the meeting itself. If it is well prepared then it has every chance of going well, but a variety of matters need attention along the way.

The way the event is viewed, by all parties, is important. Subscribe to the thought 'Success doesn't come to you, you go to it' (Marva Calins), and you are proceeding on the right lines; appraisal should be a catalyst to such a process. This is a working session. It is not unlike a project meeting convened to chart and ensure the progress of a particular activity – in this case the project is an individual's year's activity. The focus is on action and on improved performance in future; it is – or should be – a positive step towards success.

Appraisal has very personal, perhaps emotional, overtones as well, but regarding it as a constructive session with practical outputs is certainly the way to make it go well. It is the manager's responsibility to set the tone and to ensure, before and during the meeting, that their staff views the meeting in the right way.

Remember: an employee suffering what they feel to be a time-wasting and un-constructive appraisal will blame not the system, but their manager – and they are right so to do!

Overall approach apart, success comes not from some magic formula, but from the detail. Bear in mind both the experience of the person being appraised (have they or have they not been through the appraisal process before – or perhaps done so many times?), and the relationship you have with them. If you know a person well it makes the whole process easier, yet may also make it easier to neglect preparation or formalities that help keep the meeting on track. It is also necessary to make sure you remain suitably objective in such circumstances. Next we consider some of the individual detail.

Getting off to a good start

People may well be apprehensive about so important a meeting, so getting off to a good start, and doing so rapidly, is particularly important. Key factors here include:

1   welcoming the individual and putting them at their ease

2   spelling out the agenda (this should be no more than re-capping), and describing how the meeting will be handled

3   dealing with any administrative elements, e.g. making clear the duration of the meeting, mentioning what will be recorded etc.

4   asking the appraisee for an initial comment (for instance seeking a statement of their priorities for the meeting) to set things in motion.

The intention here is to put people at their ease, set the tone for the proceedings and move seamlessly into the main agenda.

Bear in mind that a successful start is, in part, made possible by the preparation and communication that has occurred before the meeting itself begins.

Finally here it is worth noting that efforts to get off to a good start assist you as well. It can boost confidence in the first few minutes of conducting the meeting if you perceive that things are going well.

2 · ENCOURAGING DISCUSSION

Directing the meeting

Throughout the meeting your role is to direct the proceedings. It is not to do all the talking; the appraisee should always be in the position of saying most, and certainly it is not to ride roughshod over the other person. Chairmanship is necessary; you need to keep an eye on the time, control the discussion and do justice to the agenda.

Only one person can do this. If your appraisals have two, or more, adjudicators then do be sure to decide who is in the driving seat.

A key task is to prompt and encourage comment, analysis and discussion. For example, drawing out comments about personal strengths and weaknesses, about successes and failures and about the implications of everything discussed for the future.

Two skills are key here. Both are obvious, but both can also seem deceptively simple and need careful deployment. Consider these in turn.

1   Asking questions: questions create involvement, they get people talking and the answers they prompt provide the foundation for much of what makes the dialogue of appraisal useful.

But questioning is more than just blurting out the first thing that comes into your mind – 'Why do you say that?' Even a simple phrase may carry unsuitable overtones and people wonder if you are suggesting they should not have said something, or if you see no relevance for the point made. In addition, many questions can easily prove unintentionally ambiguous. It is all too easy to ask something that, only because it is loosely phrased, prompts an unintended response. Ask 'How long will that take?' and the reply may simply be 'Not long'. Ask 'Will you finish that before we meet again to discuss the project in October?' and, if your purpose was to be able to prepare for that meeting, then you are much more likely to be able to decide exactly what to do.

Beyond simple clarity you need to consider and use three distinctly different kinds of question.

■ **Closed questions:** these prompt rapid 'Yes' or 'No' answers, and are useful both as a starting point (they can be made easy to answer to help ease someone into the questioning process) and to gain rapid confirmation of something. Too many closed questions on the other hand may create a virtual monologue in which the questioner seems to be doing most of the talking, and this can be annoying or unsatisfying to the other person – especially in an appraisal meeting where the intention is manifestly the reverse. Closed questions may produce some information, but they are not the way to handle the bulk of the session.

■ **Open questions:** these cannot be answered with a simple 'Yes' or 'No' and typically begin with words like what, where, why, how, who, and when and phrases such as 'Tell me about . . .'. Such questions are ideal to get people talking. They involve them and they like the feel they give to a conversation. By prompting a fuller answer and encouraging people to explain, they also produce far more information than closed questions.

■ **Probing questions:** these take the form of a series of linked questions designed to pursue a point. Thus a second question that says 'What else is important about . . .' or a phrase like 'Tell me more about . . .' get people to fill out a picture and can thus produce both more detail, and answer the 'why?', which lies beyond more superficial answers. Some issues may take three or four linked questions to tease out a satisfactory total response. If so, so be it − the job is to get to the crux of matters. This is an important point and a simple example may serve to illustrate. A first question may fail to get to the root of the matter: 'Why was it that deadline was missed?' ('We had to delay so that we had the agreement of all the departmental heads.') Further questions can probe further: 'Why was their agreement slow coming?' ('It really had to be sorted face to face and a meeting that everyone could attend just took ages to fix.') – 'Was there anything that could have been done to get it fixed sooner?' ('Well, I suppose I could have started the whole process earlier. . .'). Now after three questions we may be getting to the root cause. Maybe a better way of planning action ahead is needed, or maybe the person needs to be more assertive in fixing things with the more senior people with whom they must liaise. Attention here can get much more from the appraisal process than a more superficial approach.

Again an example like this makes clear the importance of preparation and of managing the meeting to get what you want from it within a reasonable time.

A warning: it is very easy to act, perhaps unwittingly, in a way that influences the comments and answers you prompt and the discussion that ensues. For example, just a tiny preliminary remark can produce this effect. Consider remarks like:

- 'You certainly had a problem with X, what do you think you did wrong?'
- 'I think X was excellent, how do you feel it went?'
- 'X has always been a problem, how did you get on with it this last year?'

All the above, and many others along similar lines, act to condition the response received. Maybe excessive defensiveness is triggered, when a less pointed question, one prompting a less emotive response, would lead into a much more constructive dialogue.

It is important to give sufficient time to the process of finding out. It may also be important to give the clear impression to staff that sufficient time is being given to something. This indicates the importance with which an issue is regarded; spending insufficient time suggests a lack of concern. For example, you could say: 'I want to go through this thoroughly, we can take an half an hour or so of the meeting on development and, if that proves inadequate, we can set another time to come back to it. Let's see how we get on.' .

Alternatively you might specify a particular stage to be reached or aspect to be dealt with, specifying – and agreeing – what will be left for later discussion.

If questions produce answers, then you must always listen to them.

2 Listening: this is most important. As has been said, the appraisal meeting is primarily an opportunity for the appraisee to have their say. In a well-conducted appraisal they should always do more of the talking than the appraiser, and the interview must not only be conducted on this assumption, but to facilitate it happening.

Asking things is one thing. Listening is something else – it needs addressing as an active process. It needs working at. Your staff wants a manager to be a good listener. In every aspect of their job managers need to be good listeners. The dangers of proceeding on assumptions, inaccurate information, or a lack of it, should be clear to us all. It is partly a matter of courtesy and partly a matter of credibility – you will never be felt to be taking something seriously if you appear unwilling to listen. Nowhere is this more true than in the sensitive environment of the appraisal interview. So care is especially necessary.

A misunderstanding here is not just a momentary inconvenience or annoyance, it can potentially effect the whole tone – and outcome – of the meeting; and thus an appraisee will see it as impacting upon their future.

The following points highlight, in checklist style, how listening effectiveness can be ensured. You should:

■ **Want to listen:** this is easy once you realise how useful it is to the communication process.

■ **Look like a good listener:** staff will appreciate it and if they see they have your attention feedback will be more forthcoming.

■ **Understand:** it is not just the words but the meaning that lies behind them you must note.

■ **React:** let people see that you have heard, understood and are interested. Nods, small gestures and signs and comments will encourage the other person's confidence and participation – right?

■ **Stop talking:** other than small acknowledgements, you cannot talk and listen at the same time. Do not interrupt.

■ **Use empathy:** put yourself in the other person's shoes and make sure you really appreciate their point of view.

■ **Check:** if necessary, ask questions promptly to clarify matters as the conversation proceeds. An understanding based even partly on guesses or assumptions is dangerous. But ask questions diplomatically, do not say 'You didn't explain that properly', and clarify immediately – this is not the sort of discussion that you want at cross purposes even for a moment.

■ **Remain unemotional:** too much thinking ahead – however can I overcome that point? – can distract you.

■ **Concentrate:** allow nothing to distract you. Look at the other person: nothing is read more rapidly as disinterest than an inadequate focus of attention. Note particularly key points: edit what you hear so that you can better retain key points manageably (you should have explained to the appraisee that you will be doing so).

■ **Avoid personalities:** do not let your view of a member of staff distract you from the message.

■ **Do not lose yourself in subsequent arguments:** some thinking ahead may be useful; too much and you suddenly may find you have missed something.

■ **Avoid negatives:** to begin with clear signs of disagreement (even a dismissive look) can make the other person clam up and destroy the dialogue.

■ **Make notes:** do not trust your memory, and if it is possible to do so, ask permission before writing their comments down.

Listening successfully is a practical necessity if you are to maximise the opportunity of any appraisal.

Remember the old saying that – 'God gave us two ears but one mouth for a good reason'.

Focus on performance

During the bulk of the interview you should keep primarily to performance factors. It should certainly not be your intention to indulge in amateur psychology or attempt to measure personality factors.

The first principle here is simply practical. You will do better talking about specific (and if possible recent) events, rather than taking too general an approach. Saying 'Of course, your time keeping always leaves something to be desired' is most likely to prompt a rebuttal (more so if it seems to be said sarcastically) – at worst it will produce the pointless 'No I'm not/yes you are' of table-tennis argument. If you stick to specifics, or at least lead in from them, then you are more likely to prompt a review – 'Let's think about deadlines for a moment, what happened on the X project?' Note that the longer ago an incident to be discussed was, the more specific facts will need to be and the worse the recall of the details will be.

Similarly you will do best at keeping the discussion constructive if you do not use emotive language. It is better, for example to talk about things being improved, rather than being bad or wrong and needing to be corrected. Similarly more or less of something is better than just stating that the current situation is wrong.

Keep personalities out of things, remember that being a bad time-keeper, say, does not make someone a bad person; focus primarily on activities.

A balance is necessary here, though of course there is also merit in calling a spade a spade. But as weaknesses are sometimes the easiest thing upon which to focus, it is easy to fall into the trap of being so much doom and gloom that the only likely response is defensive, and constructive thought goes out the window.

The safest route into negative areas is usually open ended questions that invite the appraisee to identify the less good things themselves – 'How do you think the X project went?'

After all, the worst disasters do not really need dressing up, they are well known.

More difficult perhaps are marginal areas, or things where the weakness is not recognised. Here particularly the job is to prompt recognition rather than simply say 'I'm telling you'. Only when there is a real acceptance of a fault can action to correct it be embarked on with commitment. The technique of reviewing a situation with general questions about what happened – 'what happened with X?' – and then asking why things took a particular turn – 'so why do you think you got that reaction?' – in a way that prompts the appraisee to see the lesson is a good one. What people believe they have discovered for themselves, they are more likely to retain and act upon.

Here we need to examine the appraisal system which, after all, is designed to keep the discussion on track and to provide an out-line agenda for it. Whatever your attitude to the system (and some will feel it is an albatross they are stuck with), you should use it. Most systems and most appraisal forms act as a guideline to the meeting, i.e. working through the form systematically will ensure most of what needs to happen actually does happen.

3 · USING THE SYSTEM

It is not the purpose here to specify exactly how the measurement aspect of appraisal systems should work. You may, in any case, not have the option of using other than what your organisation specifies (though you might resolve to influence things in order to instigate changes for the future). However, the measurement principles of any system do need to be clear to those who will be appraised, and that is essential to communicate to them.

The basis used can vary, but usually incorporates some form of rating scale. Topics chosen for measurement must be pertinent, and primarily that means they must be linked to the improvement of future performance, and be seen to be relevant.

As an extreme example of the wrong approach, I recall once being shown, by a course participant, an appraisal form that seemed to me inappropriately lengthy. It was described to me as being thorough. An examination soon showed that it listed many topics for discussion and measurement that seemed to me unnecessary; indeed impossible. One sticks in my mind. It seriously suggested that 'Honesty' be rated on a ten-point scale. Now I do not know about your organisation, but in mine you are either honest – or you are fired! And it is not a subject to debate at appraisal time. This takes being thorough to ridiculous length. The right things need to be selected for measurement, and then an appropriate rating scale utilised.

Five basic approaches are most common, and of course these are not mutually exclusive, they can be used in various combinations. They are:

1   **A simple numeric scale:** 1–6, 1–8 or whatever (an even number with no mid-point is favoured by many to avoid the temptation to mark everything 'average' which

can lead to an avoidance of commitment and action by providing a 'safe' mark); such could equally be designated A, B, C or similar.

2   **A descriptive scale:** this may, or may not, be linked to numbers and the words may or may not be chosen with precision, e.g. excellent, very good, good, fair, adequate, unsatisfactory.

3   **A graphic scale:** this is effectively just a line with identified positive and negative ends, perhaps with scale marks (e.g. mid or quarter points) along its length.

4   **A comparative scale:** which might be a list of say 4–10 statements, e.g. phrases like 'better than most in the group'.

5   **A behavioural scale:** this rates a list of alternatives that specifically relates to things done, e.g. something being always, almost always, usually, infrequently or never done.

Ratings are important.

The overall 'score' element of the ratings is important, but it should not obscure the fact that essentially they are there to prompt action where necessary, and that role is paramount.

They ensure consistency and fairness, something that is useful to point out to appraisees as part of the overview that explains the appraisal process and procedures to them. At a meeting always tell people the basis of assessment: and spell this out clearly (with reasons clearly identified if necessary). Make it clear that, as much as for any other reason, ratings are there for their benefit. Once discussion has been conducted, and judgements have been made, you need to be firm about decisions made. At the end of the day you are the manager and taking a decisive view, though one that is fair and reflects the facts.

4 · AGREEING ACTION

Appraisals should logically create agreed action. This may relate to overall plans, for instance setting targets for the ensuing operational period. It may also specify one-off events, such as a follow-up meeting to set up and initiate some training.

In every case be careful to:

- Make sure action points are agreed
- Make clear who will do what
- Specify, and again agree, timing
- Organise any recording of commitments in writing to be done by either party.

Do not leave loose ends here. Just one vague promise – 'Oh, let's talk about that later' – then forgotten may end up as the one thing that really sticks in the appraisee's memory – 'That's the trouble with appraisals, lots of fine promises – then nothing!'

A good summary, worthwhile action to follow and everything cut and dried are the hallmarks of a satisfactory ending to the meeting.

> *Keep a good eye on timing throughout the meeting. Running short of time and rushing towards the end can dilute the effectiveness of the whole event.*

Conclusions

At the end of the meeting there may be mixed feelings. There has been praise, but there may well have been need for less positive comment as well. The net out-turn should always be positive. You should end on a positive note almost whatever the circumstances, and make a firm link to the future. Specifically:

■ Recap and note any action points that are agreed.

■ Deal with any points of documentation, for example saying what either party should put in writing.

All done? Not quite: final words should always include a thank you to the appraisee for the part they have played in the process (and for their work during the last year!). If there is one word that sums up the tone of the ending of the meeting, it is surely that it should end on a note of encouragement .

IN SUMMARY

There is a good deal to remember here, and to some extent success is very much in the details, but certainly overall keys to success are to:

- Keep the meeting on track and focus its discussion appropriately

- Respect the agenda and the formats involved

- Get the appraisee talking and encourage openness

- Balance discussion of strengths (and how to build on them) with weaknesses (and how to correct them) and of past performance and future intentions

- Aim for a constructive discussion and an action-orientated outcome.

Next we turn to more detail about the areas of discussion that make up an appraisal interview.

5 · Areas for Discussion

Deciding the topics to address, their respective priorities and how to approach them.

In this Chapter:

1 DECIDING WHAT TO ASK

2 PHRASING QUESTIONS APPROPRIATELY

3 GETTING PEOPLE TALKING

4 LINKING TO THE SYSTEM

Appraisal is about assessing past performance and prompting good future performance. That said, what exactly does the discussion deal with? Two things act to focus discussion. First, the system itself, which will identify many of the topics on which discussion is expected to touch. Secondly, the job itself – and to an extent, of course, the events of the period to be assessed – will also affect the detail.

Thus every job will dictate certain areas for discussion. A sales responsibility, for example, has a very direct link with sales results and the link between work activity and those financial results will constitute a major part of the review. While every job is different, every appraisal scheme is normally designed to cover a number of different jobs around an organisation. Some tailoring is therefore likely to be the norm, but certain items are likely to crop up, at least as a basis for what is discussed, as common factors.

> *Always check topics on standard forms and rule out areas that are not relevant to particular individuals before, not during the meeting.*

1 · DECIDING WHAT TO ASK

Common questions

Certain general questions may be useful in their own right, and useful also to enable you to lead conversation from the general to the particular. For example:

- What elements of your job are you best at?
- What do you enjoy most about your job?
- What areas of activity do you think need review?
- What one thing would help you do your job better in future?
- How would you suggest we can we improve communications between us?
- Are there any people you find it difficult to get on with?
- What was the worst problem you experienced in the last (six months)?

Questions like these, followed if necessary by that unfailingly useful question 'why?', can be prepared ready to deploy and prompt a significant part of the discussion. A sequence of questions can be used to direct discussion in specific directions, for example:

- What elements of your job do you enjoy most?
- Why is that?
- What makes you cope with this so well?
- Could your skills in that area be better used?

In addition, a more direct route to many specific issues will be needed.

2 · PHRASING QUESTIONS APPROPRIATELY

The shape of the meeting normally falls into two distinct parts:

1   A review of past performance
2   Intentions for the future.

Each of these is highlighted in turn, both in terms of the kind of headings under which discussion may be organised and examples of the kind of questions that each needs.

Review of past performance

The natural starting point is some general overview questions, both because they act as icebreakers and because they genuinely open up the discussion and get us into the process, for example:

- What do you hope to get from this meeting?
- On what areas do you suggest we spend most time? (this in context of the agenda)
- Overall how do you feel about your last year's activity?

Then the focus can be turned to more specific topics:

Your job and its tasks

- What has been the main intention in your job this last year?
- How has your job changed/developed?
- What was most challenging (difficult, frustrating etc.)?
- Which actions have influenced results most?
- If there have been problems, can you identify causes?
- How do you feel about the year (was it interesting, fun etc.)?

Relationships with other people

- Who have been your main contacts this year?
- Which relationships have helped your work and results most (and least)?
- How do you feel about your relationship with others?

Personal reactions

- What have you learned during the year?
- What can you build on?
- What must you avoid or change?
- How would you – with hindsight – have approached things differently?

Skills/development ratio

- What are the key skills you need for your job?
- Is this changing?
- What about specific strengths and weaknesses?
- Are there ways in which you are under utilised?
- Do you have specific development needs?

Conclusions

■ What has been most important/significant to you this year?

■ Are there other matters we should discuss?

Intentions for the future

The most important aspect of the appraisal is the next (though it stems from our review of the past). Again some overall questions may provide a sensible starting point:

■ How will your job change – need to change – in the coming year?

■ What improvements can be made?

■ What are the priorities for action?

■ Will your working relationships extend or change? If so how?

Your job and tasks

■ What are the specific challenges for next year?

■ How will you approach them?

■ Is there additional support that would help you achieve more?

■ What new problems do you anticipate (and how can they be overcome)?

■ What specific objectives need setting and how should success be measured?

Relationships with other people

■ How can existing relationships be strengthened?
■ What new relationships must be created?
■ What link is there between your skills and your ability to work with others?

Personal reactions

■ How do you see your role developing in future?
■ How does that relate to your long-term career plans?
■ What steps will take you in the right direction?
■ Does the future look appealing?

Skills/development ratio

■ What development action is necessary to allow you to perform satisfactorily and achieve what is required of you next year?
■ What skills should development address?
■ When – and how – should development needs be addressed?

Conclusions

- How do you feel this meeting has gone?
- Are there final questions or points you wish to raise?
- Are any follow-up sessions necessary/desirable? (if so they should be specified and scheduled)
- What are you main objectives for next year?
- Can you achieve them?

This kind of approach must reflect the individual job. Thus many such questions will focus on more individual issues, for example development may link skills (say, report writing) and projects that demand their use. The approach should also fit with any standard format used within the organisation. It must also be practical. For example: it must not be so long, detailed or nit-picking and complicated that doing it justice within a sensible amount of time is impossible. It must address issues that are practical and sensible to discuss. I mentioned earlier a company appraisal form that measured 'honesty', giving it ratings like other factors on a list running from 1–10. This takes being thorough to ridiculous lengths and thus makes a good point.

The trick is to limit the topics for discussion to make them all manageable, and focus them so that they genuinely highlight key issues.

3 · GETTING PEOPLE TALKING

Questioning technique is important (and was dealt with in the last chapter). Other factors however also influence people's willingness to enter discussions and do so openly. These include:

■ **Their readiness:** which goes back to all that was said about preparation in Chapter 2.

■ **The relationship they have with you:** it will be difficult to make appraisal very different to other interactions, so if you never succeed in getting someone to open up, they are unlikely to suddenly do so at an appraisal meeting. The right ongoing relationship fosters a good appraisal style. This is also affected by others who may be present.

■ **The corporate (or departmental) culture:** both parties being comfortable with the process which means that a satisfying appraisal almost always makes the next one easier to conduct and more constructive. The success of the process thus can breed success in a way that may have wide ranging effects (e.g. an improvement of staff retention).

■ **The environment:** comfortable surroundings certainly help (see Chapter 3).

There is one overriding factor which contributes to success and that is the attitude that you take. There is an awful American maxim which says that if you can fake the sincerity, everything else is easy. Not so; staff can detect an uncaring manager at fifty paces. If you really care, if you want to make the appraisal process constructive, and want to create an environment in which good work is done and people thrive, then this drives the process like nothing else. Where this is the case it always shows.

Adopt a positive attitude yourself and make this show, remembering that enthusiasm for the process and the future is contagious.

4 · LINKING TO THE SYSTEM

In reality these kinds of question need to flow from the agenda suggested by the appraisal system, and very often by the appraisal form. This needs to be central to both your preparation and your conduct of the meeting.

One useful way of putting yourself in a position to direct the meeting surely is to annotate a copy of the form itself (another clean copy can be completed later). This means that you have both the formal information, and notes about your plan and planned questions conveniently in front of you on single sheets. As the appraisee will also have used the form to help them prepare, this can be a useful trick to help make sure you are both singing from the same song sheet.

IN SUMMARY

The conduct of the meeting itself is not complicated in the sense of being intellectually taxing. All the individual elements of it and all the things that must be done are straightforward. But it is something of a juggling trick. The successful meeting will:

- Be well prepared
- Demand, and benefit from, concentration
- Only work if you are flexible (you cannot be entirely slavish in your following of an agenda)
- Work with the system, not against it
- Utilise the carefully considered and deployed appraiser's communication skills
- Treat the whole thing in a constructive manner.

It is such factors as these that together can create and maintain a suitable focus, deal with the complexity and make the juggling act possible.

6 · Ending with a Balanced Assessment

Dealing with good and bad, but ending on a balanced note with an eye on the future.

In this Chapter:

1 ACHIEVING AN APPROPRIATE BALANCE

---

2 MAKING IT A MUTUALLY USEFUL EXPERIENCE

---

3 IMPROVING FUTURE PERFORMANCE

Achieving balance sounds attractive, but it is not simply an end in itself. Practical issues hold sway too. Take the classic issue of strengths and weaknesses. A 'balanced' meeting might be described as one that gives equal measure to both. Certainly a meeting where detailed discussion about weaknesses seemingly becomes a fixation, and any time being taken to look at strengths is effectively ruled out, is not very satisfactory. Strengths need time spent on them too; it may well be possible to achieve a far more positive effect on performance by building on strengths, than by worrying about weaknesses.

At the same time weaknesses do dilute performance and need to be addressed. The facts of the matter – the mix of strengths and weaknesses exhibited by an individual – will dictate the balance. Compromise may still be necessary, and you may find yourself trying to create opportunities to focus on some areas, and control and limit discussion of others in order not to allow a meeting to become inappropriately skewed.

The psychology here is important alongside the facts. You need to ask yourself how people will feel about the meeting given a particular mix of content and emphasis. There may be negative things to discuss, but at the end of the day the job is to send someone away resolved to work in particular ways to achieve next year's objectives. They need to be enthused, motivated and encouraged. The difficulties need dealing with, but the net effect must be right. This is always true, even of a poor performer, unless you have reached a stage at which you decide to end their employment. The job here is to combine the addressing of issues that are causing difficulties, and not fudge doing so, with the overall balance and motivational effect desired.

At the end of the day people will not actually thank you for glossing over difficulties. They want to perform well, be successful (and have this acknowledged), if something is hindering this it is best dealt with, even if the process of dealing with it is momentarily awkward. Better that than a further whole year made difficult in some way by the same factor.

1 · ACHIEVING AN APPROPRIATE BALANCE

Achieving the right balance and being able to end a meeting with both parties able to look back on it and rate it as good and useful goes, unsurprisingly, back to your preparation. In setting up the meeting, compiling the agenda, and thinking through how you will direct it, you need to consider several aspects where balance needs to be created. These include the following.

Strengths and weakness

This is a particularly important balance to get right. It seems that often managers find it almost irresistible to focus too much – perhaps exclusively – on weaknesses. The fact is that, while some appraisals are going to be predominately concerned with weaknesses because it really does reflect the needs of an individual, most need to take in both.

It is a fact that, looked at purely in terms of potential improvement, the greatest change may well be brought about by working to enhance and better use someone's strengths than by correcting weaknesses. In reality what happens is that weaknesses will probably always be addressed, and the danger is that the constructive process of building on strengths is neglected, or omitted, along with the potential advantages that this can bring. What is needed therefore is a positive intention to deal with weaknesses in a way that does not take up all the time, and to include adequate time for things positive.

Balance here will directly affect what changes the appraisal can prompt; and will ensure a much better motivational outcome as well.

Successes and failures

The situation here is very similar to strengths and weaknesses, as above. In part it is a question of doing justice to the successes. What motivational advantage can be gained from their discussion and from positive comment about them? What can be learnt from the activity and approaches deployed that made something successful? You do not want a conversation to deteriorate into what is solely a dual praise session – 'I think this was really good!' – 'Yes, well done indeed, it certainly was!' Motivational comment may – will – be useful, but so too is some real analysis.

Nothing being said here should be taken to suggest that difficult situations should be ducked. Weakness, indeed problems of any sort, should be firmly addressed – head on – if there are to be improvements.

2 · MAKING IT A MUTUALLY USEFUL EXPERIENCE

Making sure that the other person does most of the talking is necessary both for reasons of effectiveness and motivation. Clearly people are not going to find their appraisal satisfying if they are not able to get a word in edgeways. More so if the main thrust of the meeting is critical; they will want to state their case and will feel that not being able to do so is both frustrating and, worse, unfair.

Beyond that the reason for balanced inputs is essentially practical: only by getting the appraisee to talk can relevant matters
be given a suitable airing, can analysis proceed and action be
successfully prompted. Of course you have things to say, and
your guiding input and your comment and advice is important,
but this balance is key. People 'unable to have their say' are
never going to either be satisfied or view matters in a way
that will ensure their future commitment to action.

3. IMPROVING FUTURE PERFORMANCE

The danger here is that a fixed look to the past can take on
the feeling of a witch hunt. People feel such a meeting is a
long catalogue of past events (often past misdemeanours)
and query how it can possibly help in future, when future
issues seem excluded.

Ultimately, the whole reason for appraisal is to improve
future performance. A review of what has been happening

is, of course, an important part of this, but it should always be seen as a means to an end and not an end in itself.

Handled this way the lessons are much more likely to stick and action is more likely to be secured.

Long and short term issues

Here the balance should favour the immediate future. In most organisations the financial year is the main measure here, though this can vary with the field or industry involved (if your company builds aircraft an 'immediate' project may encompass five years – and more). Normally looking too far ahead creates problems with the length of time a meeting will take. It may make the discussion unmanageable; introducing too much for review for it to be reasonably kept in mind.

On the other hand, a noticeable corner needs to be set aside for longer term issues, and some of these should be career ones rather than job ones. Again a good mix here makes for a more satisfactory outcome for both parties.

The focus on job and career

To some extent these go together. There may be two ways of linking day to day activity to careers:

A general link is made. When discussing someone's report-writing skills, say, a comment might be made to the effect that an improvement here would not only sign off current projects better, but stand the person in good stead almost whatever they do in their future career (in or beyond the organisation).

A more specific link is made, usually between two things: 'If you can get your report-writing skills up to scratch then we can involve you in X, and that is a real step towards your getting a re-grading and wider responsibilities.' Or, better still, put the advantage to them first: 'A real step towards a re-grading and your getting extended responsibilities would be for you to get your report-writing skills up scratch.' It may seem a chore, but it is worthwhile. You would certainly have no problem then getting involved in X.

Remember that the inclusion of an adequate element of 'career' content will certainly appeal to the appraisee, it is to be recommended therefore in part as one of those things that act to make the appraisal process acceptable.

These can only be commented on one at a time and the danger is that they are endowed with too great a degree of separateness. The task of the appraiser is to achieve an overall balance, one that allows the practical elements of appraisal to be seen through, and one also that makes it a satisfying experience for those being appraised.

The appraisee's overall feeling about any appraisal must be positive (something that can include a feeling of satisfaction that a difficulty has been dealt with and is, if the right action is taken, unlikely to cause further problems).

There are factors here that can easily cause the wrong impression, indeed the wrong outcome, but the overriding factor is again one of opportunity; these are factors which, well handled, make appraisal very worthwhile in every respect.

Pulling it together

The other issue here is one of summary. Condensing and encapsulating everything that has gone on during a two/three hour meeting is a real skill. The job is not to reiterate everything. Rather it is to highlight the key things – good and bad – and especially to link everything that has gone on to action.

It is useful to combine describing action, the need to do something, with a statement of personal benefit. In other words do not just say 'Right, you must do so and so.' Say what will come from it, in fact start by saying what will come from it: 'You will be firmly in line for X if you just get those reports of yours half as long and twice as readable.' Such a benefit-led statement is far more likely to be appreciated and to help to make the commitment to change stick. If this is backed up with support to make change possible, then change really should occur.

> **Remember that action must not only be specified, it must be agreed and committed to (and often this involves both of you). Only then are the chances of it occurring maximised.**

Highlighting and summarising effectively can only owe so much to preparation. This is, after all, a dynamic meeting and you cannot possibly anticipate everything that will happen. You do, however, have to remember everything that did happen when you select what key factors to pull out in summary. So, summarising is a skill that demands that you are 'quick on your feet', though it is helped by:

- Your use of the agenda (and sticking to it)
- Making notes as the meeting progresses
- The appraisal system, which very often guides you to an overview which is the essence of summary.

IN SUMMARY

A good appraisal is a balanced one. Conducting one demands that:

- Individual elements of the appraisal are well handled

- The action and motivational aspects of the event are suitably interwoven

- The end result is satisfying: that means it must be seen as necessary, useful, and fair (and more besides)

- It ends on a high note, pulling matters together, high-lighting key issues – and sending people away intent on doing well next year.

A balanced out-turn meets needs on both sides (even if sometimes aspects of this may only be truly realised later). Achieving it needs attention throughout the process.

7 · Follow Up Action

'Creating continuity and linking to action after the meeting and to further review.'

In this Chapter:

Appraising people is hard work. It demands time. It demands thought beforehand and concentration on the day. Once it is all over, what do you do? Not just heave a sigh of relief and pour yourself a large drink, there are other matters demanding your attention.

It might be worth considering whether it is appropriate to end the appraisal on a less formal note with a drink for both parties (and perhaps some more useful conversation).

1 · AFTER THE MEETING

The impact of an appraisal, both its positive and negative elements, is designed to last a long time. The next formal meeting might well be a year ahead and the impact of some comments and action may be designed to stay in mind for many years. Any link, and there are likely to be – indeed should be – many, between the formal meeting and the following operational period must be firm. They should also be promptly established.

So, there is one key initial action here: to complete promptly any documentation and confirmations that are necessary after the meeting, and to send this to the appraisee, maybe flagging any opportunity for, or agreement to, further discussion. Copies might also have to go to central departments such as Personnel. You must also bring your own file up to date ready for next time.

After a period busy with appraisals it is easy to overlook the records, but delay can make completion more difficult and time consuming; and poor records will hinder the next appraisal.

2 · MAKING COMMUNICATION WORK

The documentation clearly needs to reflect the discussion. This is not the place for second thoughts or embellishments. If any matters have been left open then they must be discussed again before being documented. Any hint that what is said in writing does not represent the tone of the meeting will be resented and may well cast doubt on the whole system. Such feelings might well be widely dissemi- nated around the organisation. So documentation must:

- Be clear and unambiguous
- Be seen to be fair (as was the meeting)
- Link accurately to the system (completing appraisal forms etc.)
- List any commitments made, dates agreed, targets set etc.
- Be factual, yet strike a suitable personal note
- Deal with both positive and negative factors (certainly negative ones should not be allowed to outweigh other appropriate comment)
- End on an encouraging note and look ahead.

Beware of letting the fact that a number of appraisals come bunched together make the documentation a chore. People do not want to feel that their appraisal is other than important, so if the opposite seems evident damage will be done. Similarly, do keep a clear note of any follow-up sessions and give them priority. A further meeting scheduled with apparent urgency, perhaps enthusiasm, during what is regarded as an important meeting, and then being delayed (or worse, ignored or forgotten) is hardly likely to produce good motivation or action.

Good written confirmation enhances the actual appraisal meeting and, in particular, reinforces the action points. The time and trouble it takes is well worth while. Note also that although other people may read such notes, the prime recipient is the appraisee and it is to them things should be addressed. While the immediate focus is clear, it is worth bearing in mind that fundamentally any such records are corporate. In other words they must take a form that is self-explanatory in your absence. If your responsibilities change, or you move on, that should not mean that someone has a poor appraisal, or that your successor struggles with conducting it, just because the record is in some personal shorthand and makes little sense.

Now let us consider the overall effect of the whole process, including the supporting documentation.

The opportunity

There really is a major opportunity here. Good communication in the form of a sensible appraisal can act directly and positively to make the chances of achieving good future results and hitting specific targets more likely. Remember that the need for people to adapt and change is necessitated, not simply by identifying and then strengthening weaknesses; there may be other reasons – in the modern world the need for individuals to change is just as likely to be because of external changes occurring in a dynamic environment. This means that some of the changes prompted by appraisal by no means reflect a criticism of anything that has been done in the past. Rather they are a planned response to changes that may have been impossible to predict, or indeed to stop occurring. On other occasions appraisal meetings must address changes which are predicted and in order to ensure that people will be ready for them. This is a point that should be made clear to staff, who otherwise may feel that appraisal has something of the witch hunt about it, despite the contrary indications.

Perhaps unfortunately, in terms of the time the whole process takes, appraisal cannot be regarded as a one-off annual event. No manager can afford to heave a sigh of relief when appraisals are over and forget about them until the next year. So it is to the question of on-going activity in this area — and its attendant communication — that we turn next.

3 · CERTAINTY OF ACTION

It is possible to think of every contact that takes place between yourself and your staff throughout the year — and every communication — as potentially an ongoing part of the appraisal process. The main part of the activity though will be additional meetings to review progress. These may be 'appraisal based', an overall review of performance, or 'project based' where the appraisal opportunity comes out of the progressing of a specific project.

In either case the situation should be flagged to members of the team. It is clearly likely to cause problems later if a discussion that a staff member takes to be very informal (and a chance to say what they think openly) is then quoted in evidence, as it were, later. If they are only aware at this later stage that the manager was noting things for appraisal purposes, this may well be resented – perhaps rightly so. Many managers will, in any case, have an ongoing timetable agreed with their staff to continue the annual review in a variety of ways over the year. Some of the discussions that make up this process will, as has been said, be arranged, and timed, well ahead. Others may take advantage of circumstances; in each case both parties must be clear about what is happening.

The same principles as have been commended so far in this chapter apply to the overall ongoing process as to its more formal manifestation. This means that matters such as giving people due notice (and thus time to think or prepare), sufficient time and avoiding interruptions are again important. At least an appraisal meeting, even if interrupted, is a formal occasion. If an impromptu ten-minute session, which might maintain the continuity of discussion and review, is rendered useless by interruptions and has to be abandoned, then the whole opportunity may be wasted and the value of the process diluted.

4 · CONTINUITY OF PURPOSE

Finally, it should be noted that there is an overlap between the appraisal process as a form of communication and other areas of management communication. These natural links actually make it easier to keep the whole process 'on the boil' as it were. The four areas below make good examples:

1   Consultation and counselling. This can occur for a multitude of reasons, and can link positively to appraisal. For example, delegation can see someone working on a project that will unashamedly stretch their skills. Supervision is arranged, perhaps with some counselling alongside it. If a project involves someone in making a formal presentation for the first time, for instance, then help with preparation and a sounding board being provided at a rehearsal stage (as well perhaps as more formal training) may ensure that the final presentation is more likely to succeed. Training is involved, support and guidance too. The whole process is constructive and surely provides an insight into someone's performance that might – also constructively – be linked back into the appraisal process and the next formal appraisal meeting.

2   Training and development. This is certainly tightly associated with appraisal, indeed a prime reason for holding appraisals is to ascertain what training and development may be useful, or necessary, in future. Because training is often needed to extend skills or respond to new situations, rather than to correct faults the requirement for it may crop up at any time. Sometimes the need is unexpected and urgent. Thus this too is an ongoing process and overlaps with and runs parallel with appraisal. This may simply mean the two processes overlap, or it may mean they need tangible links. For example, appraisal identifies the need for training. As this training is arranged, discussions link back to appraisal and provide an opportunity to revisit earlier comments and reinforce points made. After training has taken place the same thing applies, further discussion – or indeed just a few words – can reinforce lessons. Incidentally, remember that training and development is far more than just 'sending someone on a course'. A host of actions from individual counselling to simply reading a book all contribute to the ongoing training process (so you are training yourself right now!).

> *Development, its inception and implementation, is another aspect of management that takes the form of a continuity of actions, large and small, that go on throughout the year.*

3   Motivation. The process of generating and maintaining an atmosphere of positive motivation amongst staff is important. Effectively done it makes a real difference to attitude, commitment and results. Appraisal – being appraised that is – should be motivational. One of the prime reasons for ensuring it is well carried out is to ensure this effect is achieved. As appraisal is designed to improve future performance, and high positive motivation creates the desire to want to succeed, the link is obvious. No opportunity should be overlooked throughout the formal appraisal (and informal review) process to achieve a positive motivational effect.

Motivational action by management may take a little time, but it is eminently worthwhile.

4   Feedback. All of the factors mentioned are enhanced by feedback. The discussions that take place under all these headings all assist each other. Thus, for instance: a positive training experience can lead to a subsequent counselling session being more constructively approached, and more being got from it as a result. And this in turn can build motivation. Clearly decisions about appraisal are affected by such chains of events and must not, therefore, be taken in isolation. For example, at the year end one course of action seems clear. But subsequent events change things. The basis for that decision is no longer valid. An action planned is changed and what happens next is tightly based on analysis of the current situation. The broad picture always needs to be kept in mind. Whatever else, appraisal must keep its feet firmly on the ground, it must reflect the real, up-to-date situation and it must never be allowed to be seen as a sterile, academic exercise.

5 · ASSESSING YOURSELF AS APPRAISER

One point apt to be overlooked in the process focuses on you. Appraising someone is an important task and it perhaps beholds all of us who do it to make sure it is done well. In which case a degree of introspection may be called for. In other words perhaps you ought to spend at least a few moments thought about your performance as an appraiser, as a regular part of the total process.

Ask your yourself such questions as: 'Did I . . .'

- Do more than my share of the talking?
- Listen effectively?
- Let what was said influence any preconceived ideas I had?
- Pre-empt their suggestions?
- Play the boss (prima donna) too much?
- Make it clear that future success is the most important outcome?
- Lead, where I should have only prompted?
- Discuss and seek alternatives creatively?

■ Dwell on the positive as much as – more than? – than the negative?

You might usefully produce a short checklist of these, and other, questions all designed to be used reflectively after the event. There is a skill involved as an appraiser that will improve with experience; what a little self evaluation can do is accelerate experience so long as, if your review suggests action, this is taken.

IN SUMMARY

The key things to remember here are that:

■ Appraisal does not end at the end of the formal appraisal meeting

■ Any follow-up documentation must be promptly and effectively completed

■ Follow-up commitments must be honoured by both parties (and this includes scheduled dates)

■ Appraisal does not happen in a vacuum and must never be considered in isolation

■ It should be seen as an ongoing process – and an ongoing opportunity.

Appraisal is not only an inherent part of the whole management process, but it takes place, in part at least, through many of the other processes that together constitute the full management task. Creating the right performance from people demands that you work with them in a variety of ways, and appraisal, important though it is, must never be viewed in isolation.

Afterword

Success is a science; if you have the conditions, you get the result.

Oscar Wilde

As a trainer I am loath to end anything – even the inevitably one-way communication that is a book – without returning to the beginning and pulling things together as one would in discussion. In this tight format it is unnecessary to recap the principles set out; suffice it to say that appraisal is an important area. It is difficult to imagine how anyone can be thought of as an ideal manager by their staff if their experience of being appraised is in any sense negative.

Management journals often publish polls in which staff can list what characteristics they feel an 'ideal manager' possesses. High, if not top of such lists, is that people want to work for someone from whom they learn. This is understandable; it is what prevents a job becoming repetitive and one of the factors that allows growth and challenge. The whole process of appraisal fits well with this need, and potentially there is every reason to believe that staff can find appraisal acceptable and valuable.

So, you owe it to your staff to get this area right. Doing so needs a clear view, a common understanding, a thorough and systematic approach, and a focus on your people, their objectives – and the future.

The results of the right approach are many. Appraisal is a clear route to improving motivation, and to making desired future results more likely to be achieved. At best it is something that contributes to potential excellence in all its organisational forms. Appraising your staff is an opportunity, and a major one.

This applies not just to formal appraisal meetings, but to the whole process as it takes place throughout the year.

To steal a sporting analogy – appraisal meetings are the manager's equivalent of an open goal. They represent an opportunity that must not be wasted; it is one directly linked to the success of your people – and thus to your own. If it works and works well, it will be because of the managerial strength and skill you bring to bear on it. An informed approach is the first step to maximising the opportunity.

Printed in Great Britain by
Amazon.co.uk, Ltd.,
Marston Gate.